The Honeybee

This book has been reviewed
for accuracy by

Eugene L. Lange, Ph.D.
Assistant Professor of Zoology
University of Wisconsin—Milwaukee

Copyright © 1991 Steck-Vaughn Company

Copyright © 1979, Raintree Publishers Limited Partnership

Library of Congress Number: 79-21165

        14   W   99 98 97

Library of Congress Cataloging in Publication Data

Hogan, Paula Z
    The honeybee.

    Cover title: The life cycle of the honeybee.
    SUMMARY: Describes in simple terms the life cycle of
the honeybee.
    1. Bees—Juvenile literature. [1. Bees]
I. Strigenz, Geri K. II. Title. III. Title: The
life cycle of the honeybee.
QL568.A6H54 595.7'99 78-21165
ISBN 0-8172-1256-6 hardcover library binding
ISBN 0-8114-8179-4 softcover binding

The HONEYBEE

By Paula Z. Hogan
Illustrations by Geri K. Strigenz

RSVP
RAINTREE
STECK-VAUGHN
P U B L I S H E R S
The Steck-Vaughn Company

Austin, Texas

4

The Honeybee

One sunny day, a queen honeybee leaves her hive. Other bees, called drones, follow her. The queen mates with a drone. Now she can lay eggs.

The queen flies back to the hive.
Laying many eggs is her job. She
puts one egg in each cell.

In three days the eggs hatch.
Out come larvae. Worker bees
feed the larvae.

After five or six days, workers cover the larvae cells. Inside the cell, the larvae grow into a pupa. In about ten days, a young bee comes out of the cells.

drone

Hives have only one queen.
Most other bees are workers.
Some bees are drones. Workers
are females. Drones are males.

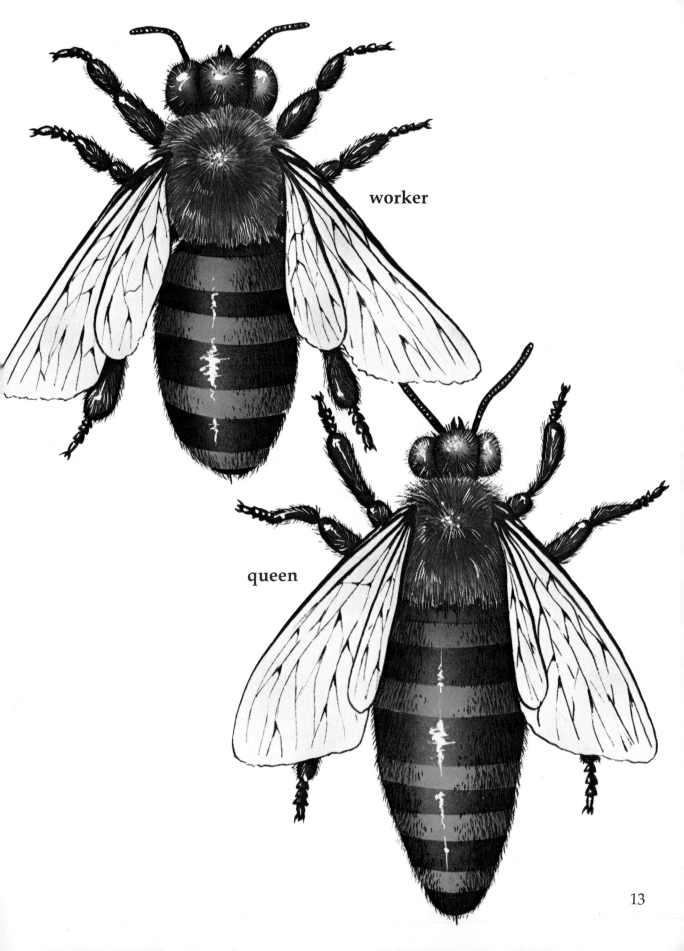

worker

queen

13

Young worker bees stay inside the hive. They clean cells and make food. Drones do no work.

Workers make wax to build
cells. Some cells are for eggs.
Other cells are for food.

Sometimes the hive is too hot.
The wax begins to melt. Worker
bees beat their wings as fast as
they can. They make wind to cool
the hive.

The door of the hive must be watched. Robber bees try to steal honey. Workers and robbers fight. Both bees die after stinging once.

Outside the hive, older worker bees look for flowers. Inside a flower is food for bees. Bees change some of the food into honey.

After finding flowers, a bee flies home. Other workers smell her food. They want to find flowers too.

The bee tells where the flowers are by dancing. The others feel her move. Now they all know where to get food.

Sometimes a hive has too many bees. The queen, some workers, and a few drones fly away. They look for a new hive. In the old hive, a new queen is born.

bumblebee

Not all bees are the same. Bumblebees build nests. Stingless bees cannot sting, but they can bite hard. Carpenter bees make homes by digging into trees.

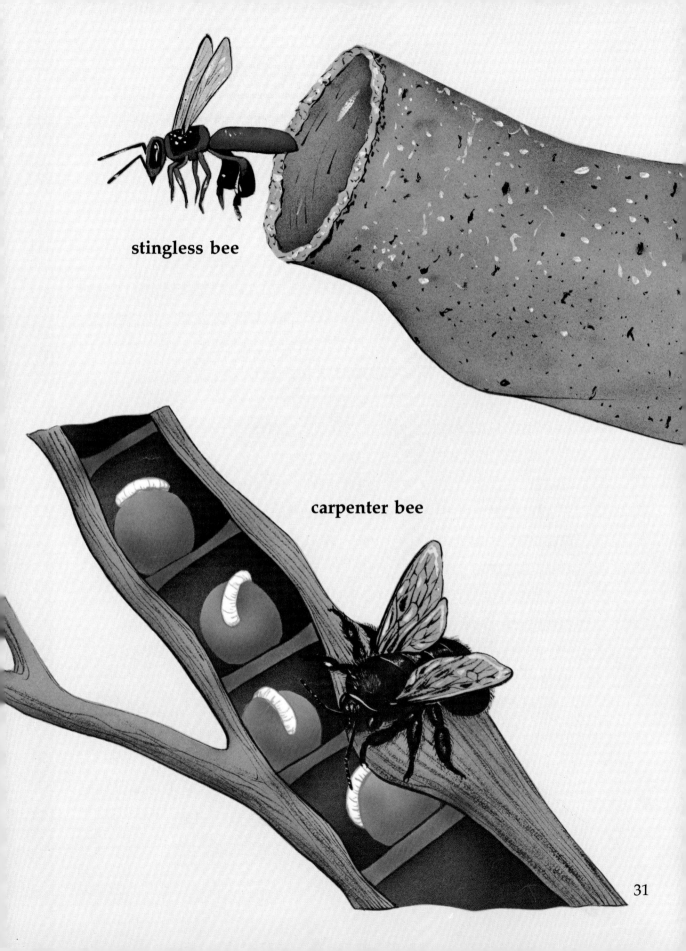

stingless bee

carpenter bee

31

GLOSSARY

These words are explained the way they are used in this book. Words of more than one syllable are in parentheses. The heavy type shows which syllable is stressed.

bumblebees (**bum**·ble·bees)—large hairy bees that build nests

carpenter bees (**car**·pen·ter bees)—bees that live alone and dig their homes in trees

cells—small holes inside the hive

drone—a male bee that does no work

hatch—eggs opening to let larvae out

hive—the home of a group of bees

larvae (**lar**·vae)—small worms that grow to be honeybees

mates—a queen joining together with a drone so she can lay eggs

queen—the only bee in a hive that lays eggs

pupa (**pu**·pa)—a larva, inside a covering, before it grows to be a honeybee

robber bees (**rob**·ber bees)—bees that steal honey from the hives of other bees

stingless bees (**sting**·less bees)—bees that cannot really sting

wax—a soft material that bees make for building cells

worker bees (**work**·er bees)—female bees that do most of the work and do not lay eggs